W9-BKB-191

MLA:
The Easy Way!
Revised Edition

Peggy M. Houghton, Ph.D.
Timothy J. Houghton, Ph.D.

Editors: Michele M. Pratt
Sandra W. Valensky

Education is one of the best investments you will ever make...and our books maximize that investment!
Houghton & Houghton

Baker College
Flint, Michigan

ISBN: 978-0-923568-95-5

www.houghtonandhoughton.com

For more information, contact:
Baker College Bookstore
bookstore@baker.edu
800-339-9879
Volume discounts are available through Baker College

LIBRARY OF CONGRESS CATALOGING-IN-PUBLICATION DATA

Houghton, Peggy M.
   MLA : the easy way! / Peggy M. Houghton, Timothy
J. Houghton ; editor, Michele M. Pratt.
      p. cm.
   Includes index.
   ISBN 978-0-923568-95-5
   1. Report writing--Handbooks, manuals, etc. 2.
Research--Handbooks, manuals, etc. I. Houghton,
Timothy J., 1961- II. Pratt, Michele M. III. Title.

   LB2369.H68 2008
   808'.02--dc22
                                          2008000949

Manufactured in the United States of America

Table of Contents

Preface

With more than thirty years of teaching experience, the authors of this handbook have learned there may be considerable confusion with writing according to the Modern Language Association (MLA) guidelines. Those who are familiar with MLA format realize that many students are apprehensive and rather perplexed with this particular writing style.

Although MLA writing style is designed for those who intend to publish, numerous colleges and universities adhere to these stringent guidelines for student papers. Years of experience have proven there are consistent questions and misunderstandings regarding the style. Consequently, this document has been developed to expand and enhance the MLA writing experience. There are some MLA guidelines that are optional; therefore, the instructor should be consulted for final authority with regard to writing assignments.

The handbook is divided into four parts. Part one focuses on the mechanics of MLA format; part two explains in-text citations; part three emphasizes the *Works Cited* page; and part four provides a sample paper.

Note: Throughout this book, both single-spacing and boldface type have been utilized. Although this is not in accordance with MLA writing style, both have been used to simply save space and/or highlight specific rules. In addition, some names given throughout are fictitious.

Part One
Mechanics of MLA

Utilizing Microsoft Word
(for applications prior to Microsoft Word 2007)

The following are specific instructions for setting up an MLA document using Microsoft Word.

Margins

All margins (top, bottom, and sides) are set at one inch. Microsoft Word allows the user to set the margin at a default of one inch. To do so, follow the guidelines below:

Margins

1. Under FILE, select PAGE SETUP.

2. Select MARGINS tab and type 1" at TOP, BOTTOM, LEFT, and RIGHT boxes. Click OK.

Alignment/Line Spacing

All documents following MLA guidelines are required to be aligned left and double-spaced throughout the entire document. Do not include additional spacing. To set the default, follow these guidelines:

Alignment/ Line Spacing

1. Placing the cursor at the start of the document, select FORMAT.

2. Under FORMAT, select PARAGRAPH.

3. Under PARAGRAPH, set ALIGNMENT to LEFT.

4. Under PARAGRAPH, set LINE SPACING to DOUBLE. Click OK.

Font Type and Size

Font Type and Size

The actual font type is an easily readable font such as 12-point Times New Roman.

To set both the font size and style using Word, do the following:

1. Under FORMAT, select FONT.

2. Under FONT, select Times New Roman.

3. Under SIZE, select 12. Click OK.

> This is an example of 12-point Times New Roman.

Paragraph Indentation

Indent the first line of each new paragraph one-half inch. This can easily be accomplished by striking TAB on the keyboard.

To set tab to a one-half inch default, do the following:

1. Under FORMAT, select PARAGRAPH.

2. Under PARAGRAPH, select TABS.

3. Under TABS, set DEFAULT TAB STOPS at .5". Click OK.

Hanging Indent

To set the hanging indent feature for the *Works Cited* page, do the following:

1. Under FORMAT, select PARAGRAPH.

2. Under SPECIAL, choose HANGING. Click OK.

> Simpson, John Henry, Thomas P. Kampou, and Michelle Knolls. *Changes in High School Theatrical Performances.* Boston: Grace, 2009. Print.

Page Numbering

Beginning on the first page and running continually throughout the MLA document, a running head is utilized. This running head appears right justified, one-half inch down from the top margin, and includes the author's last name, one space, and the appropriate page number. This can be accomplished by using the HEADER AND FOOTER function:

1. Under VIEW, select HEADER AND FOOTER.

2. Select the page number icon (the first icon on the left with the # symbol); the number will appear on the left side of the box. The cursor will appear to the right of the number. Move the cursor, using the left arrow key, to the left of the number. Press the spacebar once, thus moving the number correspondingly. Move the cursor to the left margin. At this point, type the author's last name.

Page Numbering

3. Highlight the entire typed portion, including both the author's name and the number.

4. Hit the align right key located in the toolbar.

First Page of MLA Document

At the left margin, one inch from the top of the page, the author's name, instructor's name, the course name and number, and the date are typed. Each element is double-spaced and typed on separate lines. Following these entries, the title is double-spaced and centered. Double space between the title and the first line of the document.

First Page of Document

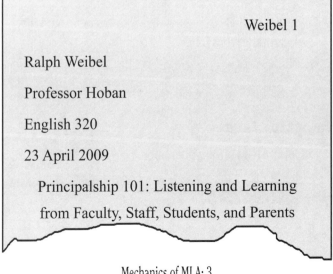

Weibel 1

Ralph Weibel

Professor Hoban

English 320

23 April 2009

Principalship 101: Listening and Learning
from Faculty, Staff, Students, and Parents

Utilizing Microsoft Office 2007 Word

The following are specific instructions for setting up an MLA document using Microsoft Office 2007 Word.

Margins

1. Select PAGE LAYOUT from the ribbon tabs.
2. Select the MARGINS icon from the PAGE SETUP drop down menu.
3. Click on NORMAL.

Alignment/Line Spacing

1. Select HOME from the ribbon tabs.
2. Select the PARAGRAPH window (by clicking the icon to the right of the word *paragraph*).
3. Under ALIGNMENT, select LEFT.
4. Under LINE SPACING, select DOUBLE.
5. Under SPACING, set both BEFORE & AFTER to 0 pt. Click OK.

Font Type and Size

1. Select HOME from the ribbon tabs.
2. Select the FONT window (by clicking the icon to the right of the word *font*).
3. Select Times New Roman.
4. Select SIZE of 12. Click OK.

Paragraph Indentation

1. Select HOME from the ribbon tabs.
2. Select the PARAGRAPH window (by clicking the icon to the right of the word *paragraph*).
3. At INDENTATION, set LEFT to .5". Click OK.

Hanging Indent

1. Select HOME from the ribbon tabs.
2. Select the PARAGRAPH window (by clicking the icon to the right of the word *paragraph*).
3. Under SPECIAL, choose HANGING. Under BY, select .5". Click OK.

Page Numbering

Beginning on the first page and running continually throughout the MLA document, a running head should be utilized. This running head appears right justified, one-half inch down from the top margin, and includes the author's last name, one space, and the appropriate page number. This can be accomplished by using the HEADER AND FOOTER function:

1. Select INSERT from the ribbon tabs.
2. Select PAGE NUMBERS in the HEADER & FOOTER box.
3. Select TOP OF PAGE and the PLAIN NUMBER 3 example.
4. Type in the author's last name and one space.
5. Double click in the document and begin typing.

First Page of MLA Document

At the left margin, one inch from the top of the page, the author's name, instructor's name, the course name and number, and the date are typed. Each element is double-spaced and typed on separate lines. Following these entries, the title is double-spaced and centered. Double space between the title and the first line of the document.

**First Page
of Document**

Ralph Weibel

Professor Hoban

English 320

23 April 2009

Principalship 101: Listening and Learning

from Faculty, Staff, Students, and Parents

Part Two
In-text Citations

The Modern Language Association (MLA) dates back to 1883. The goal of the *MLA Handbook For Writers of Research Papers* is to standardize practices for writers and researchers. This handbook is widely used among the humanities, but high schools and colleges have also accepted it as a formalized writing style for many other academic disciplines.

Guidelines for MLA in-text citations include the following:

General Comments

- Use 8 ½ by 11 inch (non-erasable type) paper.

- All pages contain a continuous running head with the author's surname (upper and lowercase lettering) followed by one space and the page number (positioned one-half inch from the top and flush with the right margin).

- Margins are one inch all around the entire document.

- Use left justification only (no right or full justification).

- Double spacing is used throughout the document. (Examples are single spaced in this book to save space.)

- Paragraph indentation is one-half inch (from the left margin).

- An easily readable type or font is used (example: Times New Roman – 12 point).

- Bold type or font is not used.

- Print on only one side of the paper (not both sides).

- Automatic hyphenating features on word processing programs are turned off.

General Comments

- *A, An,* or *The* used in the beginning of titles, organizations, and associations are ignored for alphabetizing purposes.

- *Anonymous* or *Anon* is not used (if no author is cited).

- Professional credentials, titles, affiliations, and degrees are not used (PhD, JD, MD, Sir, Lady, Saint, etc.).

- Suffixes that are essential parts of the name are included when referencing a person for the first time (Jr., Sr., III, etc.).

In-Text Citations

- The name of a news or wire service should not be used in place of the name of an author.

- Works that are cited in text list the surname of the author(s) followed by the page number(s) where the work was found (in parentheses).

Note: Credit may be provided with either a signal phrase or a parenthetical citation.

> Valensky supported the motion (54)
>
> The motion was supported (Valensky 54)

- Titles cited in text are italicized and listed in upper and lowercase lettering.

- Appropriate credit must be provided or the work may be considered plagiarized (and result in serious academic consequences).

- Everything cited in the text is cited on the *Works Cited* page. Everything listed on the *Works Cited* page is cited within the text.

Title Page

- Do not use a formal title page.

Title Page

- Cite the author's name, instructor's name, course name and number, and date in the upper left corner of the first page.

Tables

- Use sparingly.
- Use as supplemental text material.
- Do not duplicate information already in text.
- Assign arabic numerals and short titles.
- Locate as closely as possible to their mention in text.
- Include a short heading for every column.
- Use vertical spacing.
- Double space within.

Table 1

Animals Receiving Vaccinations in the United States

Year	Beef	Pork	Chicken
1998-99	11,314	10,416	876
1999-2000	12,134	10,745	912
2000-01	12,344	11,101	1,002
2003-04	13,332	12,118	1,136

Source: United States, Dept. of Ag., Natl. Center for Ag.
   Statistics; *Digest of Agriculture Statistics 2007*; US
   Dept. of Ag., Mar. 2009; Web; 12 July 2009; table 104.

Numbers

- Numerals must be spelled out at the beginning of sentences.

Nineteen eighty-four was a great year for the Detroit Tigers.

- Numerals are spelled out when only one or two words are utilized.

four	sixteen
two thousand	six million

- If the paper involves frequent use of numbers (scientific or statistical research), write numerals.

Numbers (continued)

Alaska averaged 15 students per classroom, while Georgia and Texas averaged 8 and 12, respectively.

- Write as numerals for more than two words.

7.45	93.57
607	49,670

- Commas are placed between the third and fourth digits from the right, the sixth and seventh, and so forth.

- Exceptions include page and line numbers, four-digit year numbers, and addresses.

Numbers

1,217	34,000
6,212,336	on page 2017
happened in 1999 and 2003	
located at 3112 East Tacoma	

- Write as numerals when preceding technical units of measure.

14 centimeters	2000 gallons
9 grams	21 amperes

- Write as numerals for abbreviations, times, dates, addresses, pages, and symbols.

15 lbs.	7:33 a.m.
October 22, 1939	135 12th Avenue
1313 Mockingbird Lane	page 13
$11.34	4%
5"	

- Write as numerals when comparing data.

The meat packing cooler temperature ranged from 35 degrees to 43 degrees.

- Use numbers and words in combination for large numerals.

17.5 trillion dollars	2.45 million people

- Use lowercase roman numerals for book pages numbered such as the following:

page iii	page xiv

- Use uppercase roman numerals for people's names.

Henry VIII	Milton Charles Houston IV

- Use the following for ranges of inclusive numbers. (Commas should not be used if the inclusive ranges are page numbers.)

Numbers

1-6	is used for	1 through 6
21-26	is used for	21 through 26
32-55	is used for	32 through 55
97-101	is used for	97 through 101
119-21	is used for	119 through 121
925-1,007	is used for	925 through 1,007
1,009-31	is used for	1,009 through 1,031
1,788-896	is used for	1,788 through 1,896

Page Numbers (as part of a parenthetical citation)

- Do not use *p.* or *pp.*

- Provide the second number in full for numbers through ninety-nine.

Page Numbers

2-7	is used for	page 2 through page 7
10-17	is used for	page 10 through page 17
21-32	is used for	page 21 through page 32
344-57	is used for	page 344 through page 357
593-607	is used for	page 593 through page 607
1743-55	is used for	page 1743 through page 1755

Quotation Marks

- Place quotation marks around words with special meanings or those purposefully misused.

Kelly McDonald truly believed her "internal clock" was ticking.

Michael Thurgood's "friend" turned out to be different than originally anticipated.

- Use quotation marks for translation of foreign words. (Italicize the words being translated.)

In French, the term *garder au froid* means "keep refrigerated."

Square Brackets

- Use square brackets around words that need to be in parentheses within parentheses.

The goal was to fill the stadium to capacity (for the second [night] game) so potential investors would be impressed.

Italics

- Italicize titles.

Management Innovations

Foreign Words in English Text

He was more of an *enemigo* than a friend to the Spanish authorities.

- Exceptions to this include foreign words that are well known due to frequent use in the English language. (Consult a dictionary.)

ad hoc	amigo
e.g.	et al.
genre	laissez-faire
versus	siesta

People's Names

- State a person's name fully and accurately the first time it is used, and then use only his or her last name in subsequent references unless you have two people with the same last name. If two people have the same last name, then list their names in full on subsequent references.

- Formal titles (Mr., Ms., Mrs., Dr., Professor, etc.) are not used when referring to people.

People's
Names

First Reference	Subsequent Reference
Michael James Martin, Jr.	Martin
William Jefferson Hughes, III	Hughes
Rachelle Harter-Magelli	Harter-Magelli
Edgar Allen Poe	Poe
Sigmund Freud	Freud (not Dr. Freud)

Titles of Works

- Italicize titles and use upper and lowercase lettering.

Post Modern Theory in Russia (book)

The Influence of Productivity on Job Satisfaction: A Quantitative Retail Analysis (paper)

Hamlet (play)

A Collection of Poetic Melodies (book of published poetry)

Obtaining a Boater's Safety Certificate in Iowa (pamphlet)

Exile on Main Street (compact disc)

Wall Street Journal (newspaper)

US News and World Report (magazine)

Green Acres (TV program)

Nutcracker (ballet)

Titles of
Works

Titles of Works (continued)

- Use quotation marks for titles of works published within larger works.

> "The Fiction of Marcus Gallant" (essay)
>
> "The Generation after Generation X" (article)
>
> "The Changing of the Colors" (short poem)
>
> "The Children of Carriage Valley" (short story)
>
> "The United States Economy Prior to the Industrial Revolution" (book chapter)
>
> "Jeremy Goes to College" (TV episode)
>
> "War of the Worlds" (radio program)
>
> "Brown Sugar" (song)

Titles of Works

- Do not italicize or use quotation marks for sacred writings.

- Italicize individual published editions of sacred writings.

> Bible
>
> Koran
>
> Old Testament
>
> Upanishads
>
> Gideon's Bible
>
> Upanishads: Selections for the Modern Reader
>
> Talmud
>
> King James Version
>
> Luke
>
> Talmud of the Land of Israel

- Do not italicize or use quotation marks for laws (or acts or political documents), musical compositions (identified by form, number, and key), series, societies, buildings, monuments, conferences (seminars or workshops), or courses.

Bill of Rights	John Birch Society
Empire State Building	Communication 120
NAMP Annual Convention	
Beethoven's Symphony no. 6 in A, op. 84	
University of Missouri Studies in Research Writing	
Washington Monument	

- Do not italicize or use quotation marks for words indicating the division of work.

preface	introduction
appendix	index
chapter 4	act 9
scene 8	

Quotations

Prose

- Use quotation marks and incorporate in text if quotation is four lines or less. (Quotations can occur anywhere in the sentence.)

- If no parenthetical citation is needed, punctuation is placed inside the last quotation mark.

Marisa Bernhard, in her pamphlet, *The World is an Oasis,* wrote the thought-provoking line, "We view the world not from the perception of others, but from the perception of self."

During that period, Joanna Henderson experienced "the best days of her life" and "the worst days of her life."

Quotations: Prose (continued)

- If a parenthetical citation is needed, the punctuation is placed after the citation, followed by the sentence punctuation.

> Marisa Bernhard, in her pamphlet, *The World is an Oasis*, wrote the thought-provoking line, "We view the world not from the perception of others, but from the perception of self" (12).
>
> During that period, Joanna Henderson experienced "the best days of her life" and "the worst days of her life" (32).

- Quotations longer than four lines require a colon or comma after the introductory phrase. Insert the blocked quotation (indented one inch from the left margin with no quotation marks).

- If a parenthetical citation is needed, a citation follows the punctuation at the end of the sentence.

- Doublespace the blocked text.

> Trying to encourage everyone that the world actually is a wonderful place, Bernhard noted:
>
>> The times may seem troubling, but they are actually an opportunity for improving life on this great planet. People of all nations can unite to overcome just about any type of obstacle they encounter. Differing cultures, societal norms, and customs actually strengthen us because they promote diversity. All people's ideas do not have to be the same. In fact, dissimilar thinking promotes the exchange of different viewpoints, which encourages the examination of differing perspectives for problem resolution. (21)

- If two or more paragraphs are quoted, the first line of each paragraph is indented an additional quarter inch.

- An exception is if the first sentence quoted does not begin a paragraph, then this paragraph is not indented.

Trying to encourage everyone that the world actually is a wonderful place, Bernhard noted:

> The times may seem troubling, but they are actually an opportunity for improving life on this great planet. People of all nations can unite to overcome just about any type of obstacle they encounter. Differing cultures, societal norms, and customs actually strengthen us because they promote diversity. All people's ideas do not have to be the same. In fact, dissimilar thinking promotes the exchange of different viewpoints, which encourages the examination of differing perspectives for problem resolution. . . .
>
> This is good information . . . so use it well and prosper. This world is an oasis, so use it to your advantage. . . .(21)

Quotations: Prose

Poetry

- Use quotation marks and incorporate in text if quotation is three lines or less. (Quotations can occur anywhere in the sentence.)

- Use a slash (with a space on each side) to separate individual lines.

- Parenthetical citations (with line numbers) are placed after the last quotation mark and before the punctuation at the end of the sentence.

Quotations: Poetry

Painter's poem is framed with a sense of hopelessness: "We try in vain as time leaves us forever" (3).

Johnson ponders, "What will happen to me this night / This is my concern in such complex circumstances" (12-13).

Quotations: Poetry (continued)

- Quotations longer than three lines begin on a new line (indented one inch from the left margin with no quotation marks).

- Parenthetical citations follow the punctuation at the end of the sentence.

> Martin's "Paradise Through Flight" is very detailed and descriptive:
>
> > Elevation brings out the best in human beings.
> > Spirit rises with altitude, as troubles erode.
> > The euphoria experienced is overwhelming.
> > Complete submersion in atmospheric pleasure.
> > The soul is refreshed with a sense of newness and purity. (5-9)

Drama

- Set off quotation from the text for two or more characters in a play.

- Begin the dialog next to the character's name (all capital letters, indented one inch from left margin). Follow the name with a period, and start the dialog.

- Indent all subsequent lines of a character's dialog an additional quarter inch.

- Start a new indented line when the dialog switches to another character (following the same guidelines for the first character).

- Follow prose and poetry guidelines for other aspects of formatting.

Stephen Mandrelli's screenplay for *The Fading Sun* suggests the harshness of the pioneer environment:

> TEX. I can't sleep on freezing ground.
>
> BILLY. That's not a bad thing because many men who sleep here never wake up again.
>
> TEX. You mean they die from the cold?
>
> BILLY. The cold only makes things uncomfortable. The Indians do the killing. There's nothing worse than a Sioux brave looking for revenge in the middle of the night.

Quotations:
Drama

Punctuation (periods, question marks, exclamation points)

- Avoid exclamation points unless in direct quotations.

- All punctuation is outside of the closing quotation mark unless it is part of the actual quotation.

Original (taken from an article by Jeremy Sims)
The health care situation in the United States is such that we need to take immediate action!

Quotation
Sims assaulted "the health care situation in the United States . . . " (12).

Did Sims assault "the health care situation in the United States . . . " (12)?

Intense drama followed Sims' assault on "the health care situation in the United States . . . " (12).

Sims stated, "The health care situation in the United States is such that we need to take immediate action!" (12).

Quotations:
Punctuation

- Following are examples of periods and commas used with quotation marks:

Quotations: Punctuation (continued)

Original

I can only say that on the surface my client appears to be guilty, but evidence will show otherwise.

Quotation

Roselli noted, " . . . on the surface my client appears to be guilty, but evidence will show otherwise" (142).

Original

If you take the time to read what I have written, you will better understand my position.

Quotation

" . . . take the time to read what I have written . . . ," he told me (63).

Quotations: Punctuation

- If the quotation is a question, the question mark is placed inside the closing quotation mark.

The president then asked, "Why is the data so inaccurate?"

- If the quotation ends a sentence that is a question, the question mark is placed outside the closing quotation mark.

When does Robertson discuss "the power of the pen"?

- If the question mark occurs where a period or comma are typically utilized, the period or comma is omitted.

"Have you ever felt the need to write instead of speak?" Robertson inquired.

- Use single quotation marks to set off a quotation within a quotation.

Roselli noted, "On the surface the case appears to be an 'open and shut' one, but evidence will show otherwise."

Ellipses

- Sometimes writers omit words, phrases, or sentences from passages in order to convey information with shortened quotations.

- The resulting quotation must accurately represent the original source.

- An ellipsis within a sentence uses three periods (with a space before each and a space after the last).

- If a parenthetical citation is needed, it is placed after the last quotation mark, followed by the sentence punctuation (after the final parenthesis).

Original (extracted from an article by Bernie Polen and Thomas Eckert)
Food safety, based on the seven principles of HACCP, protects the public from pathogens in our food supply, which is of great importance to many consumers.

With ellipsis
Polen and Eckert indicate that "food safety . . . protects the public from pathogens in our food supply, which is of great importance to many consumers" (21).

- An ellipsis at the end of a sentence uses four periods (with no space before the first or after the last).

- An ellipsis at the end of a sentence with no parenthetical reference uses four periods (with no space before or after the last). An ellipsis with a parenthetical reference uses three periods (with no space before or after the last).

Original (extracted from an article by Bernie Polen and Thomas Eckert)
Food safety, based on the seven principles of HACCP, protects the public from pathogens in our food supply, which is of great importance to many consumers.

Ellipses (continued)

With ellipsis
Polen and Eckert indicate that "food safety, based on the seven principles of HACCP, protects the public from pathogens in our food supply . . . " (21).

Author-Page Citations

- Following are examples of books, magazine articles, or journal articles with single authors (cited in text or in a parenthetical reference).

Wyman noted that The Rolling Stones are truly one of the greatest rock bands ever (152).

The Rolling Stones are truly one of the greatest rock bands ever (Wyman 152).

- Following are examples of books, magazine articles, or journal articles with multiple authors (cited in text or in a parenthetical reference).

- Use *et al.* if the work has more than three authors.

- Spell out the word *and.*

Scholars such as McLean, Tempest, and Williams support opposing viewpoints (135-46).

Other scholars support opposing viewpoints (McLean, Tempest, and Williams 135-46).

Women were found to be more productive than men in jobs involving human contact (Sears et al. 241-43).

- Following are examples of quotations from a book, magazine article, or journal article (cited in text or in parenthetical reference).

Monte concluded that productive workers were "satisfied" and "motivated" (126), while Turgot found them to be "committed" (112).

As Simpson states, "Diversity is needed in order to achieve personal and professional goals . . . " (216).

It is likely true that "diversity is needed in order to achieve personal and professional goals . . . " (Simpson 216).

- When citing an entire work without page numbers (print, non-print, performance, or electronic publication), the title is italicized in text (rather than cited in a parenthetical reference) or simply referred to using significant individuals (authors, editors, directors, performers, etc.).

In text
Cyman's *Watchful Eyes of Society* offers compelling detail about the security of the United States.

Works Cited (for better understanding of the citation above)
Cyman, Patricia R. *Watchful Eyes of Society.* Ed. Annette
  Birko. 2006. *American Security Information Page.*
  Web. 4 Aug. 2007.

Author-Page Citations

- For multiple works by the same author (cited in text or in parenthetical reference), cite the author, title (italicized), and page numbers.

Many people experience trauma based on childhood experiences (Jones, *Psychology Today* 121-34).

In *Psychology Today*, Jones indicates that many people experience trauma based on childhood experiences (121-34).

Jones notes that many people experience trauma based on childhood experiences (*Psychology Today* 121-34).

- For authors with the same last name, use the first initial and last name (or full name) in all references.

Edward Johnson believes the surge in China's economic growth will be short lived (17).

Other economists believe China is destined to reach much higher levels of prosperity (T. Johnson 48).

Author-Page Citations (continued)

- For an unknown author, cite the full title in text or a shortened version of the title in a parenthetical reference. (Use quotation marks for article titles and italics for book, newspaper, periodical, etc. titles.)

> *In text*
>
> According to the article, "The Times are Changing, Now More than Ever," people need to make sacrifices in their careers if they hope to advance (22).
>
> People need to make sacrifices in their careers if they hope to advance ("The Times are Changing" 22).
>
> *Works Cited* (for better understanding of the citation above)
>
> "The Times are Changing, Now More than Ever." *Newsweek* 6 June 2008: 22. Print.

Author-Page Citations

- For multi-volume work cited in a parenthetical reference, cite the author, volume (with a colon), and the page(s).

- When one volume of a multi-volume set is used and the Works Cited page notes the volume, the in-text citation requires only the author and page number(s).

- For whole volume work cited in a parenthetical reference, cite the author (with a comma), and *vol.* (before the number).

- For whole volume work cited in text, write the word *volume* (before the number).

> The legal system provides justice for victims of this type of crime (Smith 3: 261).
>
> The legal system provides justice for victims of this type of crime (Smith, vol. 3).
>
> In volume 3, Smith claims the legal system provides justice for victims of this type of crime.

- For a corporate author or government publication, cite the author and page number(s).

> The United States Department of Justice reported that the Commercial Retail Workers Union (CRWU) is completely against merit based wage increases (22).
>
> A recent report stated the Commercial Retail Workers Union (CRWU) is completely against merit based wage increases (United States Department of Justice 22).

- Cite electronic or online sources like printed sources.

- Cite the author and page number(s) (although page numbers from online documents are often not available).

- Cite *par.* (before the paragraph number) in a parenthetical reference if the source uses a paragraph numbering system.

> *Electronic source with numbered pages:*
> John Brasheem reiterates the point that "the economy is based on supply and demand" (21).
>
> *Electronic source without numbered pages:*
> Response to the drug varied dramatically (Robbins).
>
> *Electronic source with numbered paragraphs:*
> Substance abuse is not limited to urban areas (Confetti, par. 4).

- For novels or plays, add helpful information such as chapter numbers (in addition to page numbers).

- Cite page number first (with a semicolon), then *ch.* (before the chapter number).

- List chapter number or a similar designation if that is the only information available. List page numbers if available.

Author-Page Citations (continued)

Nicholas Rachlinski appears in *The Money Game* as a man obsessed with wealth, yet afraid to take any of the risks necessary to achieve it (185; ch. 1).

In *The Heart Beats Slowly*, Sara Bordeen grudgingly accepts her fate in an arranged marriage (ch. 2).

Author-Page Citations

- For sacred writings (Bible, Torah, Koran, Sermons, etc.), cite the book, and separate the chapter and verse with a period.

In the Bible, Jesus states, "For God so loved the world that he gave his one and only Son, that whoever believes in him shall not perish but have eternal life" (John 3.16).

- For a personal interview, cite the person's name (in text or in a parenthetical reference).

Guitarist Jeff Beck discussed changes in his lifestyle over the past four decades.

My lifestyle had to change, or I would not be here today (Beck).

Avoiding Plagiarism

Plagiarism is a growing problem in educational institutions both domestically and internationally. The word *plagiarize* is defined in *Merriam Webster's Collegiate Dictionary* (10th edition) as, "to steal and pass off (the ideas or words of another) as one's own" (888).

Plagiarism can take one of two forms: intentional or unintentional. When a writer knowingly uses other authors' works without providing appropriate reference citations, he or she is intentionally plagiarizing. If, on the other hand, a writer uses others' thoughts or ideas and does not realize that credit must be provided, he or she is guilty of unintentional plagiarism. Unfortunately, both types of mistakes can result in serious academic consequences. When plagiarism occurs, some institutions may require that the student receive a failing assignment grade; others may insist on a failing course grade; others may place the student on academic probation; and, in extreme cases, some institutions may actually expel the student.

It is incumbent on the writer to be forthright and honest with regard to using original and/or existing writing. Plagiarism can be easily avoided if the writer simply provides appropriate credit when borrowing ideas or citing directly from another individual's work.

When paraphrasing (rewording) work from another author, the writer must provide credit to the person who developed the original work. This simply acknowledges the fact that the paraphrased material was the work of another individual. It is not primary data (original); rather it is secondary data (information already in existence).

Avoiding Plagiarism

Likewise, when citing a direct quote, appropriate credit must be given as well. Again, this signifies that the quote is provided by another individual. When citing verbatim (using another person's exact wording), the borrowed material must be placed in quotation marks and properly cited.

Part Three

The Works Cited Page

Every MLA document should include a works cited section at the end of the document listing all references. Every reference cited in the text should be listed on the Works Cited page, and every reference listed on the Works Cited page should be cited in the text.

References allow readers to find and utilize sources cited in text. References also indicate the vigilance of the writer, so particular attention should be paid to details (spelling, punctuation, publication dates, accuracy, etc.). Most importantly, references give proper credit to authors for their work.

Guidelines for the MLA Works Cited page include the following:

General Comments

- Use 8 ½ by 11 inch (non-erasable type) paper.
- The heading is *Works Cited* (centered, in upper and lowercase letters).
- All pages contain a continuous running head with the author's last name followed by one space and the page number (positioned one-half inch from the top and flush with the right margin).
- Margins are one inch all around the entire document.
- Use left justification only (no right or full justification).

- Entries are double spaced between and within. (Examples are single spaced in this book to save space.)
- An easily readable type or font is used (example: Times New Roman – 12 point).
- Bold type or font should not be used.
- Print only on one side of the paper (not both sides).
- The first line is flush left, with the following lines (if any) indented one-half inch (hanging indent).
- Automatic hyphenating features on word processing programs are turned off.

General Comments

- Entries are listed in alphabetical order by authors (using surname of first author, followed by surname of second author, etc.), associations (if the work is authored by an organization), or titles (if the author is unknown or the work is anonymous).
- *A, An,* or *The* (introductory words) in titles, organizations, and associations are ignored for alphabetizing purposes.
- *Anonymous* or *Anon.* is not used.
- Professional credentials, titles, affiliations, and degrees are not used (PhD, JD, MD, Sir, Lady, Saint, etc.).
- Suffixes that are essential parts of the name (Jr., Sr., III) are included after the given name, preceded by a comma (Hartness, Andrew T., Jr. or Saad, Michael James, III).
- Titles are italicized and in upper and lowercase lettering.

Numbers

Numbers

- Titles beginning with a numeral are spelled out.

"Three Cheers for Joe Stiver's Market Beating Strategies"

Page Numbers

- For numbers within a range, write the second number in full through ninety-nine.

- Page numbers are listed as follows:

1-9	is used for	page 1 through page 9
12-19	is used for	page 12 through page 19
33-42	is used for	page 33 through page 42
249-56	is used for	page 249 through page 256
492-503	is used for	page 492 through page 503
n. pag.	is used for	No pagination given

Page Numbers

- Do not use *p.* or *pp.*

- Do not underline or italicize.

Abbreviations

- Acceptable abbreviations for months are the following:

Jan.	is used for	January
Feb.	is used for	February
Mar.	is used for	March
Apr.	is used for	April
May	is used for	May
June	is used for	June
July	is used for	July
Aug.	is used for	August
Sept.	is used for	September
Oct.	is used for	October
Nov.	is used for	November
Dec.	is used for	December

Abbreviations: Months

Abbreviations (continued)

- For United States cities, spell out the city and omit the state.

New York	is used for	New York, New York
Detroit	is used for	Detroit, Michigan
Chicago	is used for	Chicago, Illinois
Princeton	is used for	Princeton, New Jersey

- For Canadian cities, add the abbreviated province if the city is not familiar.

Toronto	is used for	Toronto, Ontario, Canada
Windsor, ON	is used for	Windsor, Ontario, Canada

- For cities outside the United States and Canada, add the abbreviated country if the city is not familiar.

London	is used for	London, England
Manchester, Eng.	is used for	Manchester, England

Publishers

- In general, give only enough information for the reader to look up the publisher. For example, use Houghton for Houghton Mifflin Co. However, if (1) writing a bibliographic study or (2) history is important to the paper, list the publisher's name in full.

- Omit *A, An*, and *The* when used as an introductory word in a publisher's name.

Daniels	is used for	The Daniels Co.
Atlas	is used for	An Atlas Company
Runkel	is used for	A Runkel Firm

- Omit *Corp., Co., Inc., Ltd.*, and *LLC*.

Gale	is used for	Gale Research, Inc.
Johnson	is used for	Johnson Corp.
Bethanials	is used for	Bethanials, LLC.
Dewitt	is used for	The Dewitt Co., Ltd.

- Omit *House, Press* (use *P*), *Publishers, Book, Editors*.

Harper	is used for	Harper and Row Publishers, Inc.
Random	is used for	Random House, Inc.
U of Utah P	is used for	University of Utah Press
Simple	is used for	Simple Books
Parkins	is used for	Parkins, Chang, and Wilmore Editors

- Omit first names.

Madison	is used for	James R. Madison
Kiles	is used for	J. J. Kiles
Wiley	is used for	John Wiley
Reed	is used for	Jerry Reed and Sons

- Omit secondary surnames.

Rondeau	is used for	Rondeau and Hartness Publishers, Inc.
Harcourt	is used for	Harcourt, Brace, Jovanvich
Caterra	is used for	Caterra and Nichols Books

- Use familiar letter abbreviations instead of full publisher names.

MLA	is used for	The Modern Language Association of America
UMI	is used for	University Microfilms International
ERIC	is used for	Educational Resources Information Center

Abbreviations (continued)

- Other abbreviations:

2nd ed.	is used for	Second edition
Ed. or ed.	is used for	Editor (capitalize if beginning a sentence)
Vol.	is used for	Volume (as in Vol. 22)
vols.	is used for	Volumes (as in 3 vols.)
n.p.	is used for	No publisher or place of publication given
n.d.	is used for	No date of publication given
n. pag.	is used for	No pagination
chap.	is used for	Chapter
supp.	is used for	Supplement
P	is used for	Press
U	is used for	University
Diss.	is used for	Dissertation
Comp.	is used for	Compiler
Trans.	is used for	Translator

When Listing by Author(s)

- First, last, and middle names are used (if available).

An article authored by Michael Eugene Comos is listed Comos, Michael Eugene.
An article authored by Michael E. Comos is listed Comos, Michael E.
An article authored by Michael Comos is listed Comos, Michael.
An article authored by M. E. Comos is listed Comos, M. E.

- For one author note the following example:

> Hartness, Andrew. *Socializing on College Campuses*. Ann Arbor: U of Michigan P, 2008. Print.

- For multiple authors note the following example:

> Sienkiewicz, John Henry, Anthony P. Scarcelli, and Michael Jarema. *Great High School Athletes Transition into Coaching Roles*. New York: Harper, 2008. Print.

Note: Invert the first author's name but not subsequent authors.

- For no publication date note the following example:

> Stemmer, Michael S. *Working Hard Toward Retirement*. Detroit: United Auto Workers P, n.d. Print.

Listing by Author

- For multiple citations by the same author(s) use the following:
  - List the name(s) in the first entry only.
  - Type three hyphens in each additional entry (to represent the name or names) followed by a period.
  - List entries in alphabetical order by title.

> Peters, Barbara J., and Michael Bojelay. *Commercial Real Estate Bargains*. Chicago: Johnson, 2006. Print.
>
> ---. *Light Industrial Real Estate Bargains*. Chicago: Johnson, 2008. Print.
>
> ---. *Residential Real Estate Bargains*. Chicago: Johnson, 2004. Print.

- For multiple citations by the same first author, list in alphabetical order by the second author's surname.

When Listing by Author(s) (continued)

Talbot, Brian Patrick. *Marketing Retail Cosmetics in California*. New York: Buffalo State UP, 2008. Print.

Talbot, Brian Patrick, Mitchell Clawson, and Jeffery Peace. *Bridging the Engineering and Packaging Gap in Cosmetic Manufacturing*. New York: Buffalo State UP, 2004. Print.

Talbot, Brian Patrick, Michael T. Greening, and Jeffery Peace. *Retail Trends in California*. New York: Buffalo State UP, 2006. Print.

Talbot, Brian Patrick, and Jeffery Peace. *Packaging Technology in Pittsburgh*. New York: Buffalo State UP, 2007. Print.

Listing by Author

- For corporate, unknown, or anonymous author(s), list by the title or association.

Eastern States Public Library Association Desk Reference. New York: Signet, 2008. Print.

Encyclopedia of the Midwestern States. Chicago: McGraw, 2007. Print.

National Research Team for Drug Abuse. *Cocaine Reality in Rural America*. New York: McGraw, 2008. Print.

Nicky Hopkin's Solo Piano Projects. Berkeley: U of California P, 2008. Print.

- For unknown or anonymous author(s) with no publication date, note the following example:

Critical Reviews of John Ahern's Theatrical Performances. Austin: U of Texas P, n.d. Print.

- For unknown or anonymous author(s) with no publisher, no place of publication, or no publication date, note the following example:

> *Joe McCracken: The Richest Man East of the Mississippi.*
> n.p., n.d. Print.

Books

- Detailed entries are generally listed in the following order:
  Author(s)
  Title (italicized)
  Editor(s), translator(s), or compiler(s) (if applicable)
  Edition
  Volume(s)
  Series
  Publication city
  Publisher
  Publication date
  Page numbers (if applicable)
  Medium of publication used

Book Entry

- In general, list author(s), title (italicized), publication city, publisher, publication year information, and medium.

> Hoban, Donna M. *Medical Methodology for Combating Migraine Headaches.* Detroit: Houghton, 2008. Print.

- See the section *When Listing by Author(s)* for one author, multiple authors, no publication date, multiple citations by the same author(s), multiple citations by the same first author, unknown or anonymous author(s), unknown or anonymous author(s) with no publication date, and unknown or anonymous author(s) with no publisher or publication date.

- For an edited compilation or anthology, note the following example:

Books (continued)

Book Entry: Anthology

Frank, Donald, ed. *From Past to Present: Forty Years of Sound Distribution Advice.* Chicago: Random, 2008. Print.

- For a compilation or anthology (play, short story, poem, essay) note the following example:

Poe, Edgar Allen. "The Raven." *The World's Finest Poetry.* Ed. Brice Drogasch. Cincinnati: U of Cincinnati P, 2006. Print.

- For a translation note the following example:

Terry, Lisa Ellen. *The Sander's Codes.* Trans. Don Lewandowski. Highland Park: Kreissl, 2006. Print.

- For an edited edition note the following example (1974 is the original publication date and 2007 is the edited edition date):

Book Entry: Edition

Danielson, Lillian Mae, ed. *The Real Story Behind Viet Nam.* By James Treblune. 1974. Iowa City: U of Iowa P, 2007. Print.

- For an edition note the following example:

Tranchida, Peter J. *Practicing Law in Michigan.* 2nd ed. Detroit: Wayne State UP, 2008. Print.

Book Entry: Volume

- For one volume note the following example:

Prohaska, Paul. *Formulas of a Master Sausage Maker.* Ed. Thomas P. Eckert. Vol. 7. New York: Cambridge UP, 2008. Print.

- For two or more volumes note the following example:

Mitchell, Riley. *The American Encyclopedia of Professional Hockey.* Ed. Brett T. Houghton. 3 vols. East Lansing: Michigan State UP, 2007. Print.

- For a series note the following example (12 is the series number):

> Hemler, Erin M., ed. *Learning the Art of Ballet*. Learning the Art of Dance 12. Ann Arbor: U of Michigan P, 2008. Print.

- For page numbers note the following example:

> Jagger, Michael P. Afterword. *The Life of a British Rock Star*. By John Sapienza. Chicago: Harmony, 2007. 243-51. Print.

- For a signed article in a familiar reference book note the following example:

> Lapensee, Dennis L. "Planet Earth." *Encyclopedia Britannica*. 27th ed. 2008. Print.

- For an unsigned article in a familiar reference book note the following example:

> "Plantation Soil." *Encyclopedia Americana*. 2007 ed. Print.

Brochures and Pamphlets

- In general, list like a book.

> Boston Symphony. *The Music of Jason Stein*. Boston: Barnes, 2008. Print.
>
> *Food Safety at Home*. Ann Arbor: NSF, 2008. Print.
>
> Audobon Society. *Wild Birds of North Carolina*. Raleigh: Johnsonville, 2006. Print.

Government Publications

- In general, if the author, editor, or compiler is known, list first. If the agency bears more importance, the author, editor, or compiler is placed after the title.

Government Publications (continued)

- If the author, editor, or compiler is unknown, list the issuing government agency first.

- Conclude with the title (italicized), publishing city, publisher, publishing year, and medium.

England. Ministry of Agriculture. *Food Security Threats Within*. London: MPO, 2007. Print.

Pennefather, Michael Martin, comp. *Catalog of FDA Staphylococcus Publications, May 4, 1991-July 20, 2006*. Washington: GPO, 2008. Print.

United States. Dept. of Education. *Education Variances in Public Schools*. Washington: GPO, 2007. Print.

United Nations. *Manufacturing Progress in Developing Nations*. New York: McGraw, 2008. Print.

Published Proceedings of a Conference

- In general, list like a book with added significant information.

Somerset, Daniel S., and Anthony Randazzo, eds. *Proceedings of the Forty-Ninth Annual Meeting of the Supernatural Phenomenon Society, June 11-16, 2006: Open Discussion Session*. Albuquerque: Parker, 2008. Print.

Published Dissertations

- In general, list like a book with significant information added before the publication facts.

- Use *UMI* if published by University Microfilms International.

> Parnello, James A. *The Influence of Post Traumatic Stress on African American Korean War Veterans.* Diss. U of Florida, 2006. Ann Arbor: UMI, 2003. Print.

Unpublished Dissertations

- In general, enclose title in quotation marks without italicizing.

> Sauls, Patrick K. "A Comparative Study of CEO Ethics in Non-Profit Organizations." Diss. U of Missouri, 2006. Print.

Journals (with continuous pagination throughout annual volumes)

- Do not punctuate after listing the journal title.

- In general, list the author(s), article title (in quotation marks), journal title (italicized), volume number, publication year (in parentheses), page numbers, and medium.

- Ignore issue numbers, seasons, and months in journals if pages are numbered continuously throughout every annual volume (as most are).

- See the section *When Listing by Author(s)* for one author, multiple authors, no publication date, multiple citations by the same author(s), multiple citations by the same first author, unknown or anonymous author(s), unknown or anonymous author(s) with no publication date, and unknown or anonymous author(s) with no publisher or publication date.

> Andrews, Christine A. "What is the True Meaning of Spousal Psychological Warfare?" *Marriage and Counseling Review* 12 (2007): 389-401. Print.
>
> Hendrix, James Marshall. "An Analysis of Change in Pop Music Culture." *Journal of Contemporary Music* 21 (2008): 253-67. Print.

Journals (without continuous pagination throughout annual volumes)

- Some journals do not number pages continuously through every annual volume, choosing instead to begin each issue on page one.

- In general, follow the guidelines for journals (with continuous pagination throughout annual volumes), but add a period and the issue number after the volume number.

> Marcelli, Linda M. "Gender Stereotypes in Manufacturing." *Journal of Management* 14.3-4 (2007): 14-21. Print.
>
> Mickelberry, Claude Charles. "A Comparative Analysis of Leadership Styles." *Leadership Quarterly* 13.2 (2006): 112-19. Print.

Journals

Journals (using only issue numbers)

- Some journals do not use volume numbers, choosing instead to use issue numbers only.

- In general, follow the guidelines for journals (with continuous pagination throughout annual volumes), but treat issue numbers the same as volume numbers.

> LeFrank, Kathleen L., Susan Mary Trainer, and Cheryl Querfeld. "The Influence of High School Relationships on Adulthood Friendships." *Journal of Social Commentary* 21 (2006): 119-32. Print.

Journals (with a serialized article)

- Some journals publish serialized articles or a series of articles in multiple issues of one journal.

- In general, follow the guidelines for journals (with continuous pagination throughout annual volumes), but list all information in one entry for the same author(s) and title.

Hagen, Sandra L., and Karen Ann Kernosek. "Situational Factors in Long Distance Relationships: A Qualitative Analysis." *Journal of Communication Research* 21 (2007): 321-33; 22 (2007): 17-26, 96-107. Print.

Microfiche

- Start with original publication information. Add source title (italicized), volume, year (in parentheses), identifying numbers, and medium.

Stein, Jason. "OSHA Tightens Regulations in Welding Shops." *Baltimore Gazette* 23 Nov. 2006, late ed.: B17. *NewsBank: Safety Reforms* 12 (2006): fiche 2, grids B7-12. Microform.

Reviews (of books, performances, or films)

- In general, list the reviewer (if applicable), title of review (in quotation marks, if applicable), title of the work reviewed (italicized), author (editor, translator, director, etc.) of the work reviewed, publication title (italicized), publishing date (day, month, and year), pages, and medium.

Mingles, Zachary L. "American Classics." Rev. of *Brave Hearts of Early American Pioneers,* by Anthony Zuccaro. *New Republic* 12 Aug. 2007: 23-34. Print.

Mellworth, Randy. "New Movie Roles for Television Actors." Rev. of *Bright Lights in Big Cities*, dir. Benjamin Wells. *Tallahassee Herald* 17 Jan. 2006, late ed.: D1. Print.

Rev. of *Anthology of Modern Dance*, eds. James Sellman and Gwen M. Barrett. *Times Literary Supplement* 5 Sept. 2007: 231-43. Print.

Newspapers

Newspapers

- In general, list the author (if signed), article title (in quotation marks), newspaper (italicized), publication date (complete day, month, and year), edition, page numbers, and medium.

- Do not list volume or issue numbers.

- List the city in square brackets (not italicized) if not included in newspaper name.

- Do not include introductory articles (*A, An, The*) in newspaper title.

- Add the edition (if listed) after the date.

- Do not list a wire or news service as the author; do not list *Anonymous*.

- If the article is not printed on consecutive pages, list the first page number and plus (+).

- No punctuation directly follows the name of the newspaper.

> "Delphi Plant Closing Affects Thousands." *Daily News* [Detroit] 13 Nov. 2008, late ed.: A2-3. Print.
>
> Skrock, Linda. "The Pennant Race Heats up in Boston." *Boston Herald* 28 Aug. 2008, early ed.: C1+. Print.

Editorials

Editorials

- In general, list the author (if signed), title (in quotation marks), source (italicized – newspaper, magazine, etc.), publication date (complete day, month, and year), edition (if applicable), page numbers, and medium.

- List *Editorial.* after the title (before source).

> Hardy, George. "American Teenagers and Morals." Editorial. *Newsweek* 12 Jan. 2006: 21-24. Print.

"Underage Drinking on College Campuses." Editorial. *Denver News* 14 Apr. 2008, early ed.: C4. Print.

Magazines

- In general, list the author (if signed), article title (in quotation marks), magazine title (italicized), publication date (complete day, month, and year if available), page numbers, and medium.

- Do not list volume or issue numbers.

- If the article is not printed on consecutive pages, list the first page number and plus (+).

"Careers in Veterinary Science." *Animal Welfare* June-July 2008: 16-18. Print.

Morelli, Stephanie. "New Retirement Strategies for Baby Boomers." *Money Management* May 2007: 115-21. Print.

Presnal, Peter K., and William Gates. "Website Design for Small Business." *Savvy Tech* 6 Mar. 2008: 22+. Print.

Television Series or Radio Programs

- In general, list episode or segment title (in quotation marks), significant individuals (performers, directors, narrators, producers, etc.), program title (italicized), series title (if any), network, call letters and city of station, broadcast date (day, month, and year), and medium.

"Ice Skating on Michigan Shorelines." Narr. Annie Hughes. Prod. Harmen Miller. Dir. Nicholas Bently. *Winter Sports Documentaries*. NBC. WDRQ, Detroit. 17 Jan. 2008. Television.

Music Videos

Music Videos

- In general, list performer, song title (in quotation marks), album title (italicized), manufacturer, date of song, significant individuals (director, producer, etc.), channel, date of viewing (day, month, and year), and medium.

- List *Music video* after the date of song.

> Richards, Keith. "Eileen." *Main Offender.* Virgin, 1988. Music video. Dir. Patrick Kelly Roddy. VH1. 12 June 1991. Videocassette.

Sound Recordings

- In general, list the emphasized individual (artist, composer, conductor), title of recording (italicized), performers (if applicable), date of recording (if available), manufacturer, and year of issue.

- List the medium (CD, LP, Audiocassette, Audiotape, etc.) after the year of issue.

Sound Recordings

> Ellington, Duke, cond. *Concert For the Philippines.* Duke Ellington Orch. Rec. 13 Feb. 1945. Columbia, 1979. LP.
>
> Seger, Bob. *Bob Seger's Greatest Rock Ballads.* Capitol, 2007. CD.
>
> Wilkerson, Lynn. *The Evolution of Music.* Perf. Andrew Folin and Kyle Clemmons. EMI, 1978. Audiocassette.

- For a specific song, list the song title in quotation marks.

> King, B. B. "Rollin' Stones." Rec. 12 May 1956. *King of Blues.* Chess, 2008. CD.

Film or Videos

- In general, list the title (italicized), director (producer, choreographer), performers, distributor, year of release, and medium.

Film or Videos

> *Living For Tomorrow.* Dir. Mitchell Shockey. Perf. David Reed, Christopher Cadjun, Tia Presnal, and Paul Gellstone. Miramax, 2006. Film.

Performance (concert, opera, ballet, or play)

- In general, list the title (italicized), significant individuals (playwright, writer, director, performers, etc.), performance site (theater and city), performance date, and medium.

Performances

> *Hamlet.* By William Shakespeare. Dir. Dennis Hartsig. Perf. Michael Donnell and Angela Wilmer. Magic Bag Theater, Detroit. 5 Apr. 2007. Performance.

Interviews (broadcast, published, or recorded)

- In general, list the person interviewed, interview title (in quotation marks – otherwise list *Interview* or *Interview with . . .*), interviewer may be added if known, interview source (italicized – program, publication, or recording), interview date (day, month, and year), pages (if applicable), and medium.

Interviews

> Fonda, Angela. "Running a Successful Business Interview." *Meet The Entrepreneur.* ABC. WABC, New York. 12 Aug. 2007. Television.
>
> Boscarino, Jane. Interview. *New York Times* 11 Dec. 2006, early ed.: B12. Print.
>
> Brinser, Harold. Interview with Cindy Harsbaugh. *Radio Nation.* Natl. Public Radio. WEDQ, Philadelphia. 27 May 2007. Radio.

Personal Interviews (Personal Communication)

- In general, if the researcher conducted the interview, list the name of the person interviewed and the type of interview (*personal interview, e-mail interview, telephone interview*) and the date(s).

> Eckert, J. M. Telephone interview. 23 Dec. 2008.
>
> Kilpatrick, K. K. Personal interview. 22 July 2008.
>
> Peters, Michael F. E-mail interview. 9-11 May 2008.

Lectures or Speeches

- In general, list the presenter (lecturer or speaker), presentation title (in quotation marks), meeting, sponsoring organization, presentation location, presentation date (day, month, and year), and descriptive label (*address, lecture, reading*, etc.).

> Mihalec, Alan. "Computer Systems for Newspaper Delivery." Distribution Forum. National Newspaper Convention. Palmer House, Chicago. 17 Nov. 2007. Address.

Legal Sources (acts)

- In general, list act name, Public Law number, date of enactment (day, month, and year), Statutes at Large cataloging number, and medium.

- Abbreviate *Public Law* as *Pub. L.* and abbreviate *Statutes at Large* as *Stat.*

> Transportation Equity Act. Pub. L. 105-178. 9 June 1998. Stat. 113.345. Print.

CD-ROM (non-periodical publication)

- In general, list the author (if no author, then list editor, complier, or translator if available), article (essay or poem) that is part of work (in quotation marks), publication title (italicized), editor (if relevant), edition (if relevant), publication location, publisher, publication year, and medium.

Chudzik, Stanley S. "The Real Country Near Dunsinane." *Macbeth.* By William Shakespeare. Ed. Gail Hanko. Cambridge, Eng.: Sampsell, 2006. CD-ROM.

Encyclopedia of Europe. Manchester, Eng.: McCallister, 2007. CD-ROM.

"Macaroni and Cheese Recipes." *Encyclopedia of Processed Foods.* 2nd ed. New York: Parker, 2007. CD-ROM.

Michaels, Joseph, ed. *On the Packing Room Floor.* Detroit: Gale, 2008. CD-ROM.

Sippl, Paul. *Navy Supporting Roles.* Chicago: Hartsig, 2007. CD-ROM.

CD-ROM (periodically published database)   CD-ROM

- In general, list printed source author (if available), printed source article (if available – in quotation marks), printed source periodical (italicized), volume number (if available), printed source publication date, printed source pages (if available), medium, database (italicized), vendor (if significant), electronic publication date.

Hennessy, John Thomas. "Native Americans and Teams: Qualitative Research in a Northern Michigan Casino." *Journal of Social Norms* 21 (2007): 125-29. Abstract. CD-ROM. *Periodical Abstracts Ondisc.* UMI-Proquest. Apr. 2007.

United States Senate. Committee on Fair Trade. *Report on Canadian Trade.* 13 Feb. 2006. 117th Cong. 2nd sess. CD-ROM. *Senate Masterfile.* Senate Information Service. Dec. 2007.

Internet Sites (including professional websites)

- Since readers are more likely to find web sources using author's names and titles, a URL should only be listed when necessary. For example, it should be used when the source is unlikely to be located using other information or if it is required by the proper authority.

- In general, list author (compiler, director, editor, etc.), title (italicized if independent or in quotation marks if part of a larger work), title of overall website if different than title (italicized), version or edition (if applicable), publisher or sponsor, publication date, page numbers (if available), medium (web), and access date.

- If all of this information cannot be found, list whatever is available. If there is no publisher, use *n.p.* If there is no date, use *n.d.*

Internet Sites

ABC.com. 2008. American Broadcasting Company. Web. 16 July 2008.

Advertising Institute of America. Web. 23 Oct. 2008.

Patterson's Grinders Online. 2006. Patterson's Grinders, Inc. Web. 12 May 2007.

Solarz, Michael E. *Wealth Information Page.* Web. 9 Mar. 2009.

Personal Home Pages

- In general, list creating individual, site title italicized (or if no title write *Home page* [not italicized]), date of last update (if available), medium, access date, and URL (if necessary).

Harcourt, Jeffery. Home page. 28 July 2008. Web. 15 Aug. 2008 <http://www.it.tsu.edu:6607/jeff/>.

Online Books

- In general, list authors (if no author, list editor, compiler, or translator), title (italicized), editor (compiler or translator), original publication city, original publisher, original publication year, Internet site (italicized), site editor, version, electronic publication date, sponsoring organization (or institution), medium, date of access (day, month, and year), and URL (if necessary).

- If all of this information cannot be found, list whatever is available.

Cyman, Patricia R. *Watchful Eyes of Society*. Ed. Annette Birko. 2006. *American Security Information Page*. Web. 4 Aug. 2007.

Diegel, Karen, and Lisa Shankie. *Socialist Perspectives on War*. New York, 2007. *United Women for Justice* Ed. Janet LaLonde. 2007. U of Oregon. Web. 27 May 2008.

Goldendoodle Dog Breeding. Chicago: Hartsig, 2007. *Goldendoodle Promotion Project*. Ed. Marie Chaldecott. Vers. 1.1. 2007. Goldendoodle Research Collection, Indiana State U. Web. 13 Oct. 2008.

Winfield, Antoine, and Julius L. Jones. *Gridiron Magic*. Comp. Anthony K Romo. Dallas: Houghton, 2007. *Football Scenarios*. Ed. Cedric Griffin. 2008. National Football League. Web. 6 May 2008.

Portions of Online Books

- In general, follow the guidelines for online books, but insert the title or name of the portion (in quotation marks) between the author and title.

- If the portion is a standard division of the book (introduction, foreword, afterword, etc.), insert the actual word (*introduction, foreword, afterword*, etc.). between the author and title.

Portions of Online Books (continued)

Online Books

Doyle, Darlene D., and Richard Schaefer. "Calculus."
Studies in Advanced Math. Detroit: Houghton,
2006. *Math Grant Research.* Ed. Mark Kaltz. 2007.
Florida State U. Web. 17 May 2008.

Poziemski, Jill. Introduction. *Poetry in a Bedroom
Community.* New York: Random, 2007. *American
Prose and Poetry.* Ed. Paul Novak. 2008. U of
Alaska. Web. 27 Sept. 2008.

Usler, Raymond. "Cross Country Training." *German
High School Sporting Events.* Trans. Kirk R.
Shankie. London: Doubleday, 2006. *Global High
School Sports.* Ed. Paul Hazard. 2007. U of Texas.
Web. 27 Oct. 2007.

Online Government Publications

- In general, if the author, editor, or compiler is known,
  list first (unless the agency bears more importance, then
  the author, editor, or compiler goes after the title).

- If the author, editor, or compiler is unknown, list the
  issuing government agency first.

Online Government Publications

- Conclude with the title (italicized), original publishing
  city, original publisher, original publishing year,
  medium, date of access (day, month, and year), and
  URL (if necessary).

United States. Dept. of Agriculture. Office of Food Safety
and Inspection Service. *Preventing Listeria in RTE
Meat.* Washington: GPO, 2006. Web. 27 July 2007.

United States. Dept. of Energy. Office of Natural
Resources Preservation. *Alternatives to Oil.* By
Howard L. Weinberger. 2008. Web. 24 May 2008.

> VanderHill, Donald, ed. *List of DNR Approved Consultants for Hunting Safety.* New York: McGraw, 2007. Web. 12 Jan. 2008.

Online Journals

- In general, list the author(s), article title (in quotation marks), journal title (italicized), volume number, issue number (or other identifying number), publication year (in parentheses), page numbers (paragraphs or other sections if they are numbered), medium, access date, and URL (if necessary).

- See the section *When Listing by Author(s)* for one author, multiple authors, no publication date, multiple citations by the same author(s), multiple citations by the same first author, unknown or anonymous author(s), unknown or anonymous author(s) with no publication date, and unknown or anonymous author(s) with no publisher or publication date.

> Dickerhoff, Lori. "Age Factors in Marriage." *Marriage and Family Quarterly* 11 (2008): 112-23. Web. 23 Sept. 2008.

- If the journal is from a database, state the database (italicized).

> Roddy, Juliette K. "Economics of Northern Michigan Indian Tribes." *Native American Review* 21 (2007): 291-304. Academic OneFile. Web. 15 July 2008.

Online Scholarly Project

- In general, list the title (italicized), editor (if available), publication year, sponsoring organization (or institution), medium, access date, and URL (if necessary).

Online Scholarly Project (continued)

Reconstruction of the Edmund Fitzgerald Tragedy. Ed. Pelka T. Torte. 2008. U of Minnesota. Web. 13 Sept. 2008.

Online Newspapers

- In general, list the author (if signed), article title (in quotation marks), newspaper (italicized), publication date (complete day, month, and year), medium, access date, and URL (if necessary).

Shackelford, Molly. "Waste in American Grocery Stores." *New York Times on the Web* 14 June 2007. Web. 16 June 2007.

Wilson, Daniel G. "Computer Programs for Tax Preparation." *Detroit News* 7 Oct. 2008. Web. 14 October 2008.

Online Magazines

- In general, list the author (if signed), article title (in quotation marks), magazine title (italicized), publication date (complete day, month, and year if available), medium, access date, and URL (if necessary).

Edgeworth, Thomas P. "Turning Sales Ideas into Profit." *Newsweek.com* 23 Oct. 2007. Web. 3 Jan. 2008.

Sims, Bernice. "Calculators for High School Students in Advanced Math." *Education and Technology Online* Jan. 2007. Web. 25 Feb. 2007.

Online Reviews (of books, performances or films)

Online
Reviews

- In general, list the reviewer (if there is one), title of review (in quotation marks, if there is one), *Rev. of* title of the work reviewed (italicized), author (editor, translator, director, etc. if available) of the work reviewed, online source (italicized – newspaper, magazine, etc.), review date (day, month, and year if available), medium, access date, and URL (if necessary).

Neilson, James M., and Donald St. Pierre. Rev. of
  Friends Forever: How Rugby Changed My Life, by
  Thomas Diem. *Albuquerque Times Online* 12 July
  2007. Web. 18 Sept. 2007.

Wilhelm, Jeffrey L. "Superheroes of Classic Rock."
  Rev. of *American Destiny: The English Musical
  Invasion,* ed. David Knapp. *London Book Review*
  23 Aug. 2007. Web. 20 Jan. 2008.

Online Anonymous Articles

Online
Articles

- In general, list article title (in quotation marks), online source (italicized – newspaper, magazine, etc.), publication date (complete day, month, and year), medium, access date, and URL (if necessary).

"Global Warming Affects Local Polar Bears." *Alaskan
  Gazette* 26 May 2007. Web. 13 Nov. 2007.

"Happier Days in Iraq." *Worldnews.com* 26 Mar. 2008.
  Web. 20 Apr. 2008.

Online Editorials

Online
Editorials

- In general, list the author (if signed), title (in quotation marks), source (italicized – newspaper, magazine, etc.), publication date (complete day, month, and year), medium, access date, and URL (if necessary).

- List *Editorial.* after the title (before source).

> "Dancing for Profit." Editorial. *Chicago Tribune* 27 Oct. 2008. Web. 13 Nov. 2008.
>
> Robichau, Regina. "Investing Takes Discipline." Editorial. *Financialwealth.com* 17 Aug. 2008. Web. 19 Sept. 2008.

Online Letter to Editor

Online
Letters

- In general, list the author (if signed), title (in quotation marks if available), source (italicized – newspaper, magazine, etc.), publication date (complete day, month, and year), medium, access date, and URL (if necessary).

- List *Letter.* after the title (before source).

> Bevac, Louis. Letter. *Alabama Herald Online* 23 Nov. 2007. Web. 1 Dec. 2007.
>
> Wellsworth, Amanda E. "Reform Our Public Schools." Letter. *New York Times on the Web* 6 May 2008. Web. 18 May 2008.

Online Interviews

Online
Interviews

- In general, list the person interviewed, interview title (in quotation marks – otherwise list *Interview* or *Interview with . . .*), interviewer may be added if known, interview source (italicized – program, publication, or recording), interview date (day, month, and year), medium, access date, and URL (if necessary).

LeVellier, Kenneth. "Problem Resolution in Family Owned
Businesses Interview." *Meet the Entrepreneur
Online.* 13 Nov. 2008. Web. 24 Dec. 2008.

Normile, Edward. Interview with Edward C. Zoldak. *American
Radio on the Web.* 12 Mar. 2007. Web. 25 Apr. 2007.

Trombley, Isadore T. Interview. *Parker Works.* 13 Oct.
2008. Web. 28 Dec. 2008.

Online Interviews

Online Television or Radio Programs

- In general, list significant individual(s), segment title
  (in quotation marks), program title (italicized), network,
  call letters of station, city, broadcast date (day, month,
  and year), medium, access date, and URL (if necessary).

Online Programs

Warszak, Alfred. "Fresh Water Issues in the Florida
Panhandle." *Natural Resource Usage Report.* CBS
Radio. WCBS, New York. 13 Mar. 2008. Web. 11
July 2008.

Online Paintings or Sculptures

- In general, list artist, piece title (italicized), published
  date, location, medium, access date, and URL (if
  necessary).

Online Artwork

Danielson, Patricia. *Perfect Human Body Display.* 2007.
Presnal Gallery, Chicago. Web. 28 Feb. 2008.

Online Poems

- In general, list author, title (in quotation marks),
  published date, medium, access date, and URL (if
  necessary).

Online Poems

Lentz, Stephen L. "The Seeds of Life." 2006. Web. 5
Jan. 2008 <http://www.rtu.edu/poetry/seeds/2006.
html>.

Online Maps

Online Maps

- In general, list title (in quotation marks), source (italicized – organization or institution), medium, access date, and URL (if necessary).

- List *Map* after the title.

> "Myrtle Beach, South Carolina." Map. *U.S. Gazetter.* U.S. Census Bureau. Web. 28 Nov 2007.

Online Cartoons

Online Cartoons

- In general, list cartoonist, title (in quotation marks), source (italicized – organization or institution), publication date, medium, access date, and URL (if necessary).

- List *Cartoon* after the title.

> Kelly, William. "The Martins." Cartoon. *Montgomery News Online.* 22 July 2007. Web. 9 July 2008.

Online Advertisements

Online Advertisements

- In general, list the advertisement, medium, access date, and URL (if necessary).

- List *Advertisement* after the ad name.

> Hiller's Miracle Carpet Cleaning Powder. Advertisement. Web. 23 Aug. 2008.

E-mail Communication

E-mail Communication

- In general, list writer's name, message title (from subject line [in quotation marks], if available), message description (including recipient), posting date, and medium of delivery.

> Cendrowski, Juliana R. Message to the author. 17 Oct. 2008. E-mail.

> Jackman, David M. "Re: Locker Partners in School." Message to Thomas J. Horton. 21 Sept. 2007. E-mail.

Part Four
Sample Paper

The following excerpts come from an article titled, *Academic Dishonesty*. They were reprinted with permission from the author, Dr. Michael E. Heberling. Some changes have been made to the original document to adhere to the MLA standards described in this handbook. Because only portions of the text have been retrieved, the reading is not verbatim from the actual article.

The paper is double-spaced with one-inch margins, though it might not appear that way in this publication due to typesetting issues.

½" margin for running head

Author's name
Professor's name
Course name and number
Date (day, month, year)

Paper title

Authors and page in parenthetical citation

Double-space entire document

1" margins all around entire document

Michael E. Heberling

Professor McDowell

English 320

8 May 2007

Academic Dishonesty and the World Wide Web

Cheating is a serious problem in today's educational system (McCabe, Trevino, and Butterfield 29). The ubiquitous World Wide Web has made it extremely easy for today's students to pirate everything from one-paragraph writing assignments to complete essays. Some students, in fact, might not even view this Internet plagiarism as being wrong. They have been raised on the premise that it is permissible to freely copy songs and movies from the Internet (another fallacy, of course), so they think that it is perfectly legitimate to copy someone else's words and ideas. They see the World Wide Web as a free and powerful source for the dissemination of knowledge, and they do not see any problem in using this free knowledge for their work. Students may think that it might be wrong to submit a complete paper that they had purchased off the Internet, but they do not see anything wrong with utilizing uncited quotations from different authors.

Has the Internet created and encouraged a new cheating tool which students can utilize? While there may never be a definitive answer to this somewhat philosophical question, there can be some educated assumptions based on existing literature. In the article, "Ten Updated Principles of Academic Integrity,"

McCabe and Pavela indicate newer students may not realize that the Internet is a relatively new resource tool (10-12). They note that it is the faculty member's responsibility to educate students about Internet etiquette as well as its proper use. Internet utilization is a wonderful resource technique, but when abused, the Internet can be discouraging and even detrimental to one's educational experience.

In "Ten Updated Principles of Academic Integrity," McCabe and Pavela indicate some faculty have almost abandoned writing assignments because cheating is so rampant (14-16). This is a disservice to the students because reading and writing are, in the author's opinion, two of the most important components of an education. To abandon writing assignments merely limits students in their academic growth and development.

Christina Stolarz wrote an article in the *Detroit News* that explored how many of today's students feel about plagiarism. One sixteen-year-old student said that she realized plagiarism was cheating, but that did not stop her from using several copied phrases from the web. What was her excuse? She needed the information for her paper but did not want to take the time to properly credit the sources. Her only concern was turning in the paper in a timely manner (1A).

A student who simply purchases or copies a complete paper from the Internet and turns it in as his or her own work deserves no sympathy whatsoever. He or she has cheated in the worst possible way and should be punished by failure of the course and/or

Article title in text

Author in text

Newspaper title in text

Page only in parenthetical citation

expulsion from the program (Simboli 21).

However, what about the student who completed substantial original research, but plagiarized by using improperly cited quotations from different sources? He or she obviously put forth considerable effort, but proper citation is still an issue. Should punishment for this particular offense be less severe?

Lastly, what about the student who attempts to give credit in an imprecise way but simply does not do enough work to establish his or her sources? For example, that student might cite a recent editorial in a local newspaper but does not list the author, editor, date, or page number. Is this a form of plagiarism, or is it just lazy writing?

While there is substantial evidence existing related to the prevalence of academic dishonesty, there is, fortunately, a silver lining. Some academic institutions have implemented a traditional or modified honor code. These codes are being incorporated in an effort to reduce the amount of cheating.

In the article, "Some Good News about Academic Integrity," McCabe and Pavela define traditional and modified honor. They state "traditional academic honor codes include written pledges that students sign attesting their work integrity . . . . Modified honor codes involve judicial roles for students that do not mandate the use of pledges . . ." (34).

McCabe and Pavela found institutions that implement traditional or modified honor codes have experienced some success. While cheating is not entirely eliminated, it is significantly reduced when some form of honor code is practiced ("Some Good News," 34-35).

Direct quotation in text

Ellipsis within sentence

Ellipsis at end of sentence with parenthetical citation

Use shortened version of title in parenthetical citation

The author is acutely aware that cheating, such as plagiarism, is not an absolute thing and cannot be resolved in an absolute way. Educators now have Internet tools, such as Turnitin.com, which enable them to detect plagiarism from the World Wide Web. Consider a scenario where Turnitin.com results indicate that student A plagiarized 60 percent of his or her paper, and student B plagiarized only 20 percent of his or her paper. Should the punishment be the same for both students?

If the answer is "yes," the assumption is that there is no relativity in plagiarism. Stealing one word or phrase is as bad as stealing an entire paper. Unfortunately, if this rationale were applied to the world outside academia, it would be like saying that stealing a candy bar is just as serious as stealing a million dollars.

If the answer is "no," there must be an attempt to find meaningful and uniform standards by which teachers can evaluate different levels of plagiarism. If every single paper graded by every single teacher could be evaluated by a percentage system such as the one used by Turnitin.com, this might be possible. But this sort of universal grading is not likely to happen in one's lifetime.

However, even resource tools such as Turnitin.com are not foolproof. For example, Turnitin.com only searches online databases and Internet resources. If students utilize both online and print resources, only those used from online sources are considered when attempting to detect any type of plagiarism. Furthermore, if the student utilizes only print resources (not online), such as textbooks, Turnitin.com might be a useless detection device.

While educators should certainly be cognizant of academic dishonesty, such as plagiarism, they also have the responsibility to first educate their students on the very concept of academic dishonesty and plagiarism. First and foremost, what actually constitutes academic dishonesty should be clearly defined for the students.

The suggestion is that instructors specifically detail, in their respective syllabi, a section titled something such as "Academic Integrity." In this portion of the syllabus, the instructor should clearly state his or her integrity expectations. Plagiarism should be defined. Further, it is encouraged that instructors note that they have access to online plagiarism detection programs (such as Turnitin.com) and that all student work is subject to submission to these various services.

Finally, the academic dishonesty issue should be discussed during the first week of every class. In *Plagiarism in Higher Education*, the United States Department of Education indicates that students who understand the meaning of academic integrity from the start of the course tend to submit much more original work throughout the entire course.

Academic dishonesty will likely always exist in some form. There are certain techniques, however, that deter the likelihood of occurrence.

Title in text

Works Cited

McCabe, Donald, and Gary Pavela. "Some Good

News about Academic Integrity." *Change* 33.5

(2000): 32-38. Print.

---. "Ten Updated Principles of Academic Integrity."

Change 36.3 (2004): 10-16. Print.

McCabe, Donald, Leonard Trevino, and Kenneth

D. Butterfield. "Dishonesty in Academic

Environments." *Journal of Higher Education*

72 (2001): 29-45. Print.

Simboli, Martin Trevor. "Plagiarism: Severe

Consequences in Academia." *Journal of*

Education 25.3 (2007): 17-28. Web. 5 Feb.

2008.

Stolarz, Christina. "Schools' New Target:

Cybercheaters – Michigan Districts Crack

Down on Web Savvy Students Who Think

Online Plagiarism is OK." *Detroit News* 2 Oct.

2005, early ed.: A1. Print.

United States. Department of Education. Office

of Postsecondary Education. *Plagiarism in*

Higher Education. Washington: GPO, 2008.

Web. 23 May 2008.

Same authors, multiple citations

Journal retrieved online

Newspaper

Government document retrieved online

Index